LATCH

LATCH

PAUL JEFFCUTT

LAGAN PRESS
BELFAST
2010

Acknowledgements
I am grateful to the editors of the following poetry journals and poetry presses where many of the poems included here first appeared: ABC Press, *Aesthetica*, Biscuit Publishing, *Carillon*, Cinnamon Press, *Crannog, Decanto,* Dedalus Press, *Gold Dust, HQ, Markings, Mobius, Poetry Scotland,* Purple Prose Press, Ragged Raven Press, *Revival, Sentinel, Silkworm, Stylus, Tamara, The Cannon's Mouth, The Frogmore Papers, Ulla's Nib* and *Ulster Tatler.*

I would also like to thank Jean Bleakney, Ciaran Carson, Daragh Carville, Mairtin Crawford, Moyra Donaldson, Ray Givans, Brian Keenan, Sinead Morrissey, Chris Nikkel, John Passey, Ian Sansom and the Writers' Group of the Seamus Heaney Centre for Poetry in Belfast.

Published by
Lagan Press
Unit 45
Westlink Enterprise Centre
30-50 Distillery Street
Belfast BT12 5BJ
e-mail: lagan-press@e-books.org.uk
web: lagan-press.org.uk

ARTS
COUNCIL
of Northern Ireland

ISBN: 978 1 904652 89 2 (pbk)
      978 1 904652 90 8 (hbk)
Author: Jeffcutt, Paul
Title: Latch
2010

for Gill Banks
1958-1987

I fitted to the latch
My hand, with trembling care
—Emily Dickinson

CONTENTS

HOMESTEAD

At the end of the abandoned lane
among stubby fields of nettles,
couch-grass and docks,
the old house squats.
A muddied cattle-trail curves
to the empty gate and wanders on.

Choked to the lintels with briars,
rotten window-frames gape:
beyond dangling slates
a sycamore where rooks refuse to nest.
Forcing thorns apart, I step in
to the parlour.

A barren grate,
the tiled mantelpiece shrouded with cobwebs
and the drained bodies of insects
that kicked their last as Jim Reeves crooned on the radio:
filthy strands embrace a deserted soldier,
in the mildew beside him a teddy's eye.

Broken tiles crunch to the thick, square sink
(where stains couldn't be erased)
and a raddled enamel cooker
its oven door clasped by bramble spikes,
still guarding against
the ungrateful child who wanted.

IN YOUR EYES

A scattering of islands.
Reefs, concealed bays
and exotic vegetation:
strange ecosystems
parted by dangerous channels.

Fishes swirl
and molluscs creep
as trenches plunge
into your remote,
protozoan dark.

DAD'S BONFIRE

Every weekend he attends
to the sacrifice:
weeds, sticks, newspapers and leaves
and weeds
hauled to the site.
Torn elbow above smudged knee,
wellyboot stirruped on garden fork,
he drags on a Player's,
strides to the heap
and flicks a match.
She peers out and sighs.
He spits in his palm, grasps the haft
and forks debris to the pyre:
first a frown, then a lip
smoulders and cackles into flame.
At last, she's ablaze.

GILL'S VALLEY

Slips the grime of back-to-backs,
pushes littered banks past my eyes
and calls softly from beyond allotments,
clack-clicking a resonant hello.

Hills curl and sway in dusk's pinlights,
eel-rich pastures defy the gloom,
with burnished forks a filagree beech
ignites the dallying sheen.

EVACUATION EAST

from a photograph at Oswiecim

Hot July day, no breeze.
We rest at last, in a grove of pines:
there's a shady little pond,
nearby a skylark sings.

Suitcases are spread around,
a broken wall of black leather,
our names printed on the outside:
one change of clothes (as instructed).

Children slink and jostle,
'watch out' screams Katerina
but it's good for them to play a little
after such a time we've had.

That soldier leans at the wire fence,
rifle cupped, not seeming to care.
Beyond, the dipping wail of a locomotive;
I smell burning.

DESERTS

I came at the call
holding my fears and wishes.
Stationed either side of the bed
we watched him for three days,
unconscious but twitching
under oxygen mask and drip.
Marge kept addressing him
in a crisp, measured voice,
as if a wayward child
slow to mend his ways.

No response. Nothing
but the insistent hiss of the tubes.
They showed us the scan,
a great blot at his left temple:
speech, swallowing and continence
astray in this barren stretch.

A tank commander
he endured desert battles,
capture and camps.
Three months of pumpkin soup in Bari,
years of hunger inside Stalag 8B:
liberated by Patton (with ivory-handled revolvers).
In Palestine, he'd been delayed for the meeting
when the Stern Gang's bomb
exploded on time.

He begins to regain consciousness
for seconds, then minutes:
the mask comes off, he tries to speak
but nothing utters from arid lips
slid down on the right, a worn-out leer.

With a keening nasal cry, he focuses on Marge:
fifty years and they don't need talk,
holding hands like sweethearts
before watchful family eyes.

I reappear with gifts:
he fingers them like strange artefacts,
puzzling for a while on my message
as if encrypted in a foreign tongue.
Opening a photo-book of deserts
I patiently turn pages for him,
hoping to kindle the resourceful heat
of his early prime, map-making
under the Saharan sun.

'Rendezvous at the fig-tree in four days time'
they laughed, jumped into jeeps
and motored past the pyramids
into the vast Western desert.
Wavy hair slicked back, sleeves rolled up on khaki fatigues,
he shone confidence in the camera's bright gaze;
now he's shrunken into Ward Six,
propped up, but weighed down
by the pillows around his head.
I kiss him goodbye: cloudy blue eyes
looking confused.

The engine starts up and my tears spring:
oh Dad ... we'd just traversed that void,
slowly gauging each other's presence.
In the grain of your workshop, wood-rich,
we fashioned a template of respect,
belated confidences offered like treasure.
Dusty tools now languish in this dumbed shed
and I must complete whatever remains,
speaking for myself.

PATIENT

Collapsed on my bunk,
coarse straw pinches up through greasy cloth.
Everything hurts. Head, guts,
skin hanging from aching bones:
is it really me?

    Her mane,
    my hands.

Scabby potato peelings
and water for weeks now.
Be still. Don't think about food.
After three years, you can hold
on a little longer.

    Dawn,
    heathland mist,
    hooves and heartbeats ...

Hemmed in by thick forest,
barbed wire and machine-gun towers;
secret radio in hut twelve
'the American advance is near'.

    Gravel, heather ...
    oaks:
    haunches, leather ...
    roan.

Conscript guards are frightened,
mostly old men and boys:
two caught creeping away last night.
The Kommandant made us dig the graves this morning.

STILL

Head hunched,
bony hands clasped,
gaunt arms wrapped under the covers:
he's laid out like a mediaeval knight,
pale and sunken cheeks scarred
from the nurse's clumsy shaves.
In the clutch of the bacterium,
pumped and emptied by machines.
But the eyes still flicker.
My Dad keeps going:
going on,
going away.

FIRST ASCENT

Fighting a falling sky,
the raven soars
from the summit,
quivering ebony jibs
whirlscaped in azure.
Ocean of crag and wind,
my hoarse cry glides to you.

Spanning granite ledges,
the bright cord tautens:
you begin to climb the gully,
our umbilical drawing you in.
Perched, I peer below,
your face sparkles into view:
route done, we're reunited.
The joy of a long way to go.

THE OFFICE OF THE CHIEF

Behind his mahogany desk
are framed diplomas and honours,
an expanse of gilding, signatures and red-wax seals
he loves to gesture towards,
sprawling back in the buttoned leather chair
as you remain standing.

All dubious, confides Leo,
especially one as a fighter pilot
in the Second World War:
grimacing, he seizes the joystick
and banking fast, twin machine-guns spurt,
then he dissolves to a pouting bambino,
waving little arms
and gaping around the cockpit.

ENGLISH AT NIGHT SCHOOL

Luigi's stubble matches the black leather,
the jacket crinkles
but his face doesn't.
Playing teacher, I beam and jest:
he grips the book like a shield,
staring into it
uncomprehending,
resentful.

WORDING

They rise like fish
from a restless deep,
scudding back between the waves:
a splash of shine.
Teetering at the water's edge,
my scooping pen
traces them for capture.
Eyeing the tidings,
mouth eager to taste,
I cast my lure.

PRANZO

Leaving Palazzo Vecchio, we're embroiled.
Florentines, umbrella's hoist,
thrusting home for pasta over damp cobblestones:
scooters jammed and honking,
a biretta sky.

Across huge tapestries
wolves are hunted down
with hounds and spears.
Beggars retrench to the great piazza;
fatigue gapes from David's eyes.

REARRANGING THE FUTURE

after Filippo Marinetti

Let's exalt sleeplessness,
the perilous leap, a roaring bonnet
tubed with serpents, mighty locomotives
snorting the horizon, brute electric moons,
black parades, the glitter of knives,
Salo.

DEATH WITH HONOUR

Your pink stockings,
pirouettes and gilded pantaloons
don't impress me.
I've turned the heads of monarchs,
galvanized priests, impregnated Pasiphae:
my mastery is sculpted.

From the meseta I watched you
for centuries, crossing the Duero
to raze medinas and lop skulls:
then you sat down at Tordesillas
and divided the world.
You can spike and spear me,
slash my ears, drink my blood:
but I remain your horned one.

HABANA CABARET

The guts of a grand hotel
stuffed with 50s Americana,
yellow-finned Chevrolet convertible
and chromed maw of Buick sedan.
The dance-floor, a protruding glitterballed tongue:
Cuban octet stuck in the throat
(sharp white suits, red bow-ties)
swinging out 'Somewhere Over the Rainbow'
to tables scattered like spittle.

In place of Lucky Luciano and the mob
indentured natives jump a generation or two,
lined white hands renting young mulattos.
A curtain call and the DJ starts,
jintero waves across the floor to *jintera*,
each confers with old, flatfooted squeeze:
sparkling, they join in ecstatic dance
and return to be yoked
to their owners.

jintero / jintera: a young Cuban hustler (male/female)

CONVICTION

A loop of rope with clenched knot,
a blindfold and fusiliers,
a blade above a block,
a hypodermic or cabled seat,
a stake surrounded by logs,
a heap of stones:
the cross.

WATCHERS

Below the reef of Hangman's Hill
two collies scurry sheep:
fleeces dart and jink through glistening fields
shoaling to a nook where poplars stand,
a slatted truck at the gate.

Forgotten on the heath,
three stare and twitch in rough seclusion.
They straggle down through scrub
to the troubling frontier:
no-mans-land.

The tardy trio streak from cover:
headlong, panting
into the mustered flock.
Bashful woollybacks:
relieved, but not safe.

SCARS

Over the handlebars I flew,
arms stretched out to greet the tarmac.
I crashed into childhood:
shrieking down coppiced lanes
legs pumping, loaf forwards
cleaving the air.
       The ground still hurt.
Beneath dislocated wrists and collarbone,
the deeper wounds:
having to risk, go too far, get hurt.
No care unless the blood flows
and then, overwhelmed.

MILK

'The milkman wants a son,
says he'll pay.'
She glanced down
'sell your baby brother?'
And sniggering
wandered away.

Kept watch from the corner.
They stood chatting by the pram,
he gave her white bottles
and a handful of coins.

Next day, swaddled,
that lump was still there.
Creeping towards the back door
a good stick in my hand,
I reached up, stretched over
and poked hard:

empty bottles crashed
from the window ledge,
streaked glass tinkling
and spattering.

SNAP, CRACKLE AND POP

I'm away ...
quick, someone's coming,
into cover behind the cans:
my jersey's beany blue.
It's a goon, shush.
She waddles, puzzled,
wire basket, dumb.

All clear, sprint the aisle;
now, hug piccalilli,
jars cool on my cheek,
inching past bottled sick.
Peek round the corner,
plenty goons but far away:
get down and crawl to the end.

High boxes, crispy and crunch,
sunrise over a sweeter land ...
There's the checkpoint,
guarded, keeps bad children in:
crouch, ready to dash,
please can I be saved this time.

'Hello, where's your mummy?'
Grabbed, I shriek and flail.
'Haven't got a mummy!'
Big goon bends down, grins
'and what's your name?'
Burst in tears of rage
'not got one', I'm cursed.

COUNTRY BOY

Dun-ye worry
litl bruv,
Er's gonna ask
an wen Er duz,
I'll shrugg 'I dunno', wat-ever tis.
Er piggy eyes'll peep (fur a secund ur too)
an I'll ave to trap that gaze,
musn't dodge it or I cud giv uz away.

'I ... dun ... no'
sez I, tongue slabberin.
Er do smirk
an turns bye,
wild yappin dogs
be skelterin roun me bonce.
Swingin back, Er grasps I at the throat
'tell me now, you worm'.

'I dun'—
Er clouts they words inside me gob.
'Little heathen,
I'll make you understand.'

BAGGAGE

Picked up and let go,
not even a wave,
I'm left in the shadows again.
You trust we'll be reunited
but I'll bob down the path,
under the radar and away—
standby or red-eye, further the better for me:
with stroller, holdall and drinks
beneath wispy coconut fronds,
a week without your sweaty palm,
what bliss.

RESIPISCENCE
(Beyond M)

Around the desert of your heart
poison flowers bloom brightly,
heavy scent drawing insects
toward sweet putrefaction.

Within the wasteland of your care
magnificent creatures
stalk and slither, sinking
fangs in mesmerised prey.

Through the interior of your hours
barren ridges and shifting sands,
cracked strata fearfully stretched
across a devouring crevasse.

Seven years,
an isle of neglect:
stranded beside you.

20.18 (GMT)

Bike and I at ease on Kington Hill:
green corn stirring in the birdsong breeze,
sun descending hazy over Bourn.
Hen pheasant flaps from a hawthorn bush,
glides away side-stabilising,
black ant traverses my petrol tank
and a space-station plummets
in slabs of sizzling debris
on Esperance, Western Australia.

UNDERWORLD

And didn't I charm them.
The board were pussycats,
we chatted over sweetmeats
then closed the deal:
just pick her up and walk right out,
no looking back.
Easy, I was on my way.

Didn't spare the horses to the border,
parked up, then into the back country.
A helluva long trek down,
deep valleys and caves: gloomy,
no wonder their time goes so slow.
I reached the barricade quite knackered
but still put on a smile:
security sneered, checked my warrant twice,
then a goon shrugged me to the place.

There she lay, lover girl:
dead to the world and so cute.
. I tiptoed close and stroked her pale skin.
Two blue eyes startled alight.
I grinned, 'c'mon kid, we're outa here':
she began to rise, but one leg still swollen from the bite
I had to guide her to the gate.
Dogs howled, security stamped our permit:
'bye-bye', smirked one, 'don't come back'.

The route out was tricky,
winding up through ravines to the pass.
We chatted about home
and what we'd do on our return:

champagne, steam baths, a feast, loads of nookie,
later we got on to decorations and disputed the drapes.

Across the river, the going got steep:
all I could manage was a hollow whistle
while she whimpered under her breath.
I wanted to wheel around
sink my head into that soft neck
and wallow: an animal curled in its lair.
But no turning back—not a glance
until over the border.
That was one tough deal.

'Oor-reey!'
Lashing from well behind
her howl roared past,
bounced off the hillside ahead
and smacked me in the face.
I staggered, head wobbling
like a sapling in a squall
and stopped dead.
Panting, I shouted back
'Eury honey, what's happened,
are you OK?'

The heavy quiet swirled up,
pitched onto my back
and stuck:
my legs began to shake,
stones stabbed into my shoes.
I started to turn my head,
bone grating over sinew
like a knife sawing through gristle.
Then a huge, curdling yell.

I didn't really see her,
just a squeezed white streak
that roared away like a shooting star.
I gaped and glared
at the plaintive speck
engulfed by cavernous gloom.
My eyes began to trickle,
I blinked:
the light was gone.

THE CLUB

It's exclusive, yet people join every day:
there's no application form,
no interview and no fee.
Enrolment only happens at someone else's behest,
it arrives unexpectedly
however much you might've prepared.

You enter an all-age community, for life.
Resignations are never accepted
as membership can only be passed
to family and close friends.
Renewals and extensions just come along
whether you're looking for them or not.
You're in the loss club:
soldiering on, day by day.

170

Window-rattling buses
pass me by
roaring along schedules:
I tick with the hands
and succumb.

Beneath my shadows
soft-featured girls amble
chattering,
brown eyes that see in
but do not linger.

TIDES

I wanted to stay later
last night
but I began to lose my bearings,
like that strange summer
of escape
to the verdant island.
Roaming the broody mountains,
switchbacks edging through the pines:
drenched and astray.

LONGANIZAS

Tottering her bar-stool,
stylish blonde sucks the lips off
suave caballero groping her arse.
Along the bar counter, conjoined,
three huge sausages:
cantering into love,
sorely used
or just looking.

TRYING TO SLEEP IN HOSTAL LA MANCHA

And a coach party arrives downstairs,
drags tables and chairs over the flagstoned floor
all shouting for *la cena*.
'But it's after midnight and my cook has gone'
the landlord protests:

they pull their pistols
and place them like knife and fork.
He brings bottles of *Tinto de Casa* and relights the stove.
Clashing glasses, they carouse:
one starts dagger throwing at a picture of a windmill,
another takes a candle and begins to stamp up stairs,
you cower a little lower in the bed.

The landlord returns with *pan* and *Pisto Manchego,*
they slurp, pausing only
to toss empties towards the corner:
he delivers a steaming tureen,
more wine and, behind the bar,
watches them gorge tomorrows' dinner.

'*Coñac*', one bellows (their glasses are charged).
'To our search for that shabby knight and squire',
they stand and drain the spirit
each drawing a finger across his throat.

ABANDONED ALONG
LA RUTA DE DON QUIJOTE

A dead kestrel,
the guts of a washing machine,
mule turds, single mattress
ripped, one black boot, carcass
of a computer monitor,
wide-brimmed wickerwork hat,
Barbie y Ken se Prometen
(box empty), olive stones,
a book on chivalry, whose name
I do not care to recall,
stamped *Biblioteca de Toledo.*

THE SPA OF TRUE BELIEF

Toning
You're anointed with eucalyptus honey,
alabaster clay and Madagascan spices,
stretched over a cedarwood rack
(built by native craftspeople)
and beaten with roasted oak staves,
inset with purified stones
from the slopes of Mount Ararat.

Rejuvenating
Bathed in biodynamic camel's milk,
you're injected with our trusty potion
of rainforest herbs, the stem cells of gentle infants
(harvested from sustainable communities
under supervision of the Red Cross)
and distillations from the reliquary.

Directions
Ideally situated
between nuclear power station
and the leprosy sanatorium.
We demand your custom.

Donna Torquemada
Administrator General.

VISITATION

Sprawling cloud,
a dank street corner:
the opening light within.

Planet-scaped faces
sparse hairlines receding,
bitumen coughs:
fag ash fluttering to the sticky carpet
kamikaze grey.

Glasses scrape,
the evening wheedles along:
dogged and awash
we're marooned
till turnout.

A stranger,
I hadn't entered another world:
it had set foot in me.

SOUTH AND WEST

I read letters from lovers
that couldn't be saved,
and mine to her:
no answer came.

Packages of rain wrap my salutation,
a lament chancing westward
across deaf continents
to broken lands that echo far from home.
Navigating the steps each night,
I throw sentences to clouds
and bribe the air with courtesy for dawn.
I have no prayer: just a shout
held in, the sound of something without voice
that seems to give spiritual light.
In the prison of countless cries
there is no sun.

Beyond her native lake
the ground was dark and cold:
she had no shelter,
stepping to a place
whose end was always near.
The voice was soft, she said
'these words may never reach you'.

Sweet silhouette,
I fixed upon the glowing sky
and whispered
'my skin dissolves in dew without your touch'.
What else could I say?

I'm travelling through the world
that lies before me, endlessly.
It starts to rain as I write this.
Mad heart, be brave.

Sources:
'The Country Without a Post Office' – Agha Shahid Ali (1997)
'Stepping Westward' – William Wordsworth (1803)

IN EMPLOYMENT

279 steps from the entrance,
116 urgent emails,
58 minutes before lunch,
13 hours until Friday,
2 phones ringing at once,
half an opportunity.

SHELL-SHOCK

The warfare at work
unrelenting.
My letter of admission
delivers release:
only water all morning, thence nil by mouth
and eight good weeks out of the fray.

In a blue floral pinafore
gathered at the neck
and white ribbed anti-embolism stockings,
I perch on the bed for hours like an expectant milkmaid:
then trundle from the ward
down to the guts of the infirmary.

Skullcapped surgeon raises my gown,
scores a nine-inch slice
across my belly and into groin
with a black magic-marker,
joking to nurse 'he humped a tree root
and took the hernia.'
Pink venflon jags my wrist,
huge syringe of cloudy liquid
pushes in ...

'Hello, hello—
this is the recovery room'.
Belly wound scorches
into chest and legs:
body seems drawn, deformed.

Trolleyed back,
each crevice in floor a dagger.
Ward nurse hooks up the painkilling drip
'it's like a caesarian', she snorts
'but you didn't get any joy'.

FLOOD

It lashes the shipyard city,
drowning rows of inky slates
and plunging to gutter seas;
leaky boots, I'm scuppered
for the long slosh home.

Good Friday's spring tide
ebbs, sweet-wrappers frothing:
darkened taxi snouts the waves
to shabby pool of tinkling light,
another for that road?
Dispatched down a laneway,
sodden memorial blooms
lie spent and wasting.

A periscope scans refugee streets,
convoys of terraces holed in action:
illustrated gables shudder
and groan, going down,
all dogs baying.

SCAPEGOAT

A black,
white, brown face
with shifty, slitty eyes:
stupid grin but cunning,
one foot in the shit
the other stirring.

Hangs around toilets
taking the air.
Danders strange boulevards
with tongues, tenets
and heresies, any shape
or colour you like.

So take up cudgels, jokes,
kerbstones, affidavits, knives,
whispers, Molotovs, memos, AK47s,
sneers, knuckledusters, tribunals
and thermo-nuclear devices
to banish the ugliest worry-goat
your pathetic radar
ever did see.

THIN-LIPPED WEASEL

In taut white gloves
I painstakingly review the scene.
Was everything ravelled, swept up,
cloaked: or could surprises reek,
seep out, betray?
Do unto me and I will you,
not now, but behind the gaze:
picking into pieces builds me up.

Spiteful?
No: just careful.
Outside my first sweetshop
all hoarded pennies gone
a bag of *hundreds and thousands* in my hand,
I opened rustling paper
and commenced the count.

SWAY

Befogged
and beyond rest,
the stern of my thoughts
seethe into the night:
ship's company alarmed,
pilot drunken, cold winds beating.

A slate dawn arrives,
scudding clouds press the horizon,
tides ebb and flow,
barometers fall and rise,
wakes follow prows
and the veering needle
seeks magnetism.

WINGS

Nearing the summit,
she lost her grip and fell.

The rope braced
but the tape slipped through:
her unleashed body
tumbled into space.

Arms extended
graceful head high
legs swept back,
the bright winter air streaming by.

Birds fled,
the rocks below spread their bulk
and drew her down,
plummeting, to earth.

Arms outstretched,
I hold.

UNPACKING

for Gill Banks

We begin to unload the garage,
a store-house crowded with leftovers
from my stranded years in rented rooms.
Nosing through piles of boxes,
the brother and I chuckle
at favourite shoes, scuffed
unfashionable and bent,
old albums (James Brown, Blondie,
T. Rex) and, best of all,
the shirts I used to boogie in.

Under heaps for the jumble and debris for the dump
we reach the big red trunk.
In the bedroom of our house
I'd sat with it, the evening before the service,
a vigil with scraps and shreds that would not rest.

Hauled out into the light
it glowers.
I turn towards Robert
(but he must have slipped away)
then back to the trunk,
heavy with rivets
at reinforced corners in black.
Struggling forward
I grasp a stiff brass latch:
creaking, the lid cleaves open.

I kneel before the trove
and unwrap jewellery,
birthday cards, snaps, quirky souvenirs,
perfume, faded tickets:
a bundle of my love letters.

Those vital moments,
that fleeted and flew away,
return their precious cargo so gently ...

Hushed, we're talking
and I caress your skin.

RAMADAN IN JEBEL SAHRO

Crystal sun-rays
speckle the stony desert
green, vermilion and blue.
Benbrahim, the Berber guide,
heads on through thorny scrub,
spare and sparse:
some succulent, loved by mules,
others bleached, ready to burn,
sparking from camp-fire to the stars.

The *ghibli* brings the dust of centuries:
Touareg roaming with their camels
in the vast debris of lost rivers,
my father struggling to lead his patrol
around enemy lines and back to base.

Sandstone ravines meander
to the deft, clay-walled, casbah,
a fertile haven on traders' routes
of salt, fruit and slaves.
The many tribes of Africa,
bloodlines joined in the children's faces:
they loiter, we dally—and play.
Curious strangers, still mingling
amid the rites of dusk.

ghibli: a dry wind that blows from the SE Sahara

ALBIE'S PHANTOM

for Justice Albie Sachs

Without me to steer it
the indigo arm of his suit flutters and swerves.
He's speaking on truth and reconciliation:
that hand an anchor (trapping his notes to the desk)
this sleeve a flag of passion
the vacant space that's rightly mine.

Long after the car bomb in Mozambique
he's told the secret agent wants to confess.
At the Commission, a chance meeting:
the agent sheepishly makes to shake,
I scream
'you've already taken me, you bastard.'
Albie pauses, then proffers:
'here, I have another one'.

MARAHAU
(Wispy Cloud and Lantern Moon)

The eerie skin of a great giraffe
enfolds constellations in its hide.
Vellum mottles to Canis Major
and Aries patchworks into Leo:
firmament and parchment,
tonight the stars compose.

Dog-years of searching,
I rode foul beasts that bucked and skirled
through Orion and the Pleiades:
erratic gyrations
and obscure glimpses
sculpting the border of illumination.

RAVEN

My animal of power appeared
on the day I returned to the mountain
(the inquest was to open nearby).
At the pass I limped from my car
and shuffled with a stick
to the start of the stony ascent
and halted.

My damaged leg throbbed
as I traced out the craggy ridge of *Crib Goch*;
serene, smiling to the lens,
you'd forged ahead on the climb.

I laid flowers on a boulder beside the path,
an insignificant blaze of yellow and red
amidst bleak millennia of glacial erosion
and mumbled,
words flown
the wind spearing my core.

Unable to keep on
and join you, afraid to return:
I slump to the broken ground
and remain.

Swooping down from the mountain
the great dark bird heads for me:
arrowing near,
glossy-black overhead,
gliding effortless beyond.
The raven's throaty cry booms out from the pass.
I hear the call.

TWILIGHT TJUKURPA

In a lost ocean of terracotta sand
bulges the blood-red shoulder
of an ancestral being
at rest.
As visitors clamber like ants,
bright sun crawls across the tussocked plain
of yellow spinifex,
scattered groves of mulga trees
still their agile leaves.
The land offers up its warmth.

Crimson biceps gather
and stretch,
ripple from a great scapula
six kilometres across:
the ants scatter and snap.
Over scarlet flanks
sunfire pulses, flares:
a conflagration scorches to the summit
and soars into a glistening sky.

Haloed in ultramarine and violet,
Uluru stands serene:
a beacon of the spirit
rooted in the earth's core.
This eager heart.

tjukurpa: foundational beliefs and spiritual truths (aboriginal)

THE CROSSING

after Philippe Petit

Between two fluttering candles
the swallowtail dances:
a lucent tightrope of guile,
balance and pixie-dust.
He's burning, not burnt.